DUBROVNIK
TRAVEL GUIDE

The Ultimate Handbook for Exploring the Adriatic Paradise from Old Town to Island Escapes

Harrison Walshaw

2024 EDITION
Full-Color

Disclaimer:

While we strive to provide accurate and up-to-date information, we make no express or implied representations or warranties about the completeness, accuracy, reliability, suitability, or availability of the guide or the information, products, services, or related graphics contained within it.

Every effort has been made to ensure that the information in this guide is accurate and up to date. However, due to the dynamic nature of travel information, we strongly advise that all details be confirmed with the relevant authorities or service providers before making any travel arrangements.

Please keep in mind that travel regulations, visa requirements, and other travel-related information may change over time. It is the reader's responsibility to stay current on travel advisories and requirements. The authors and publisher of this guide are not liable for any errors or omissions, or for any actions taken in reliance on the information contained in this guide.

We hope you find this Dubrovnik Travel Guide useful and inspiring. Safe travels, and enjoy your exploration of this magnificent destination!

Photo Credit Majaiva from Getty Images Signature via Canva

Photo Credit Emicristea/Canva

Table of Contents

Welcome to Dubrovnik..1
- *Why Visit Dubrovnik?*...*2*

Top Attractions...3
- *Dubrovnik Old Town (Stari Grad)*.............................*3*
- *City Walls*...*3*
- *Lokrum Island*...*4*
- *Fort Lovrijenac*...*4*
- *Dubrovnik Cathedral*..*5*

Planning Your Trip...6
- *When to Visit*..*6*
- *Visa and Entry Requirements*...................................*6*
- *Currency and Money Matters*....................................*7*
- *Travel Insurance*..*8*

Getting to Dubrovnik..9
- *Arriving by Air*..*9*
- *Arriving by Land*..*9*
- *Arriving by Sea*..*10*
- *Transportation within the City*................................*10*

Accommodation...11
- *Types of Accommodation*..*11*
- *Best Areas to Stay*..*11*
- *Budget, Mid-Range, and Luxury Options*..................*12*
- *Booking Tips*..*12*
- *Recommended Accommodations*...............................*14*

Essential Information..16
- *Local Culture and Etiquette:*..................................*16*
- *Currency and Banking:*..*16*
- *Health and Safety:*..*17*
- *Local Laws and Regulations:*...................................*18*

Exploring Dubrovnik...19
- *The Old Town*...*19*
- *City Walls:*...*21*
- *Stradun (Placa):*...*22*
- *Historic Monuments*...*23*
- *Museums and Galleries*...*28*

- *Local Markets*..29
Outdoor Activities 31
- *Beaches and Swimming Spots:* 31
- *Hiking and Nature Trails:* 31
- *Kayaking and Sailing:* 32
- *Day Trips to Nearby Islands* 32
Dubrovnik's Cuisine 34
- *Dubrovnik's Cuisine:* 34
- *Local Food and Culinary Traditions:* 35
- *Must-Try Dishes:* 38
- *Popular Restaurants and Cafes:* 38
- *Dining Etiquette:* 39
Nightlife and Entertainment 41
- *Bars and Pubs:* 41
- *Clubs and Nightlife Hotspots:* 41
- *Live Music Venues:* 42
- *Cultural Performances:* 43
Shopping in Dubrovnik 44
- *Best Shopping Districts:* 44
- *Souvenirs and Unique Gifts:* 44
Day Trips from Dubrovnik 46
- *Elaphiti Islands:* 46
- *Montenegro:* 47
- *Lokrum Island:* 48
- *Other Nearby Attractions* 49
Itineraries for Every Traveler 51
- *3 Days in Dubrovnik: A Perfect Weekend Getaway* 51
- *1-Week Adventure in Dubrovnik* 54
- *Family-Friendly Itinerary* 58
- *Budget Traveler's Guide* 62
Maps and Practical Resources 66
- *Attractions* 66
- *Public Transportation Maps* 68
Travel Tips and Recommendations 70
- *Packing Tips* 70
- *Language Phrases* 72

Additional Resources...76
- *Official Dubrovnik Tourism Website*........................... 76
- *Dubrovnik Museums and Galleries*............................. 76
- *Dubrovnik Public Transportation:* 77
- *Local Language Learning Apps:*................................. 77

Fun facts & interesting tidbits about Dubrovnik.....................78
- *History and Culture:*.. 78
- *Geography and Nature:*... 79
- *Architecture and Landmarks:* 79
- *Traditions and Festivals:* 79
- *Cuisine and Dining:*.. 80
- *Economy and Trade:*... 80
- *Entertainment and Media:*.. 80
- *Transportation:* 80
- *Tourism:* 81
- *Cultural Heritage:*.. 81
- *Linguistic Diversity:*... 81
- *Maritime Heritage:* 81
- *Fortified Towns:*... 81
- *Stradun Paving:* 81
- *The Sweet Delight:* 81
- *Religious Tolerance:*.. 82
- *Cultural and Political Influence:* 82
- *The Dubrovnik Symphony Orchestra:*........................ 82
- *The Legend of Orlando:*.. 82
- *Seafaring and Navigation:* 82
- *A UNESCO Treasure:*.. 82
- *The City of Festivals:* 82
- *Game of Thrones Connection:* 82

WELCOME TO DUBROVNIK

Welcome to the enchanting city of Dubrovnik, often referred to as the "Pearl of the Adriatic." This picturesque coastal city, located in the southern part of Croatia, is a destination that seamlessly blends history, culture, and natural beauty. As you embark on this journey, you will discover a world of captivating experiences and breathtaking scenery.

Dubrovnik, with its stunning Old Town surrounded by well-preserved city walls, has a rich history that dates back to the 7th century. The city has witnessed centuries of change and turmoil, from the days of the Republic of Ragusa to its role in the Yugoslav wars, and has emerged as a symbol of resilience, culture, and heritage.

This travel guide is your key to unlocking the many treasures of Dubrovnik. Whether you're a history enthusiast, a foodie, an adventurer, or someone seeking relaxation by the crystal-clear waters of the Adriatic, Dubrovnik has something to offer for every traveler.

About this Travel Guide

This travel guide is designed to help you make the most of your visit to Dubrovnik. Whether you're a first-time traveler or a returning visitor, you'll find valuable information, insider tips, and recommendations to enhance your experience.

Inside this guide, you'll discover comprehensive details about the city's attractions, dining options, accommodations, and practical travel advice. We've also included sample itineraries, maps, and local insights to make your journey as smooth and memorable as possible.

So, get ready to embark on your Dubrovnik adventure, and let this travel guide be your trusted companion as you explore this captivating city. Welcome to Dubrovnik, where the past meets the present, and where the Adriatic's beauty knows no bounds. Enjoy your journey!

Why Visit Dubrovnik?

1. **Historical and Architectural Marvel:** Dubrovnik's Old Town is a UNESCO World Heritage Site, known for its well-preserved medieval architecture, ancient city walls, and historic monuments. Stroll through cobblestone streets, visit centuries-old churches, and step back in time.

2. **Spectacular Scenery:** The city's coastal location offers some of the most breathtaking views of the Adriatic Sea. With its terracotta roofs and crystal-clear waters, Dubrovnik provides a stunning backdrop for travelers and photographers.

3. **Rich Cultural Heritage:** Immerse yourself in the local culture by exploring Dubrovnik's museums, art galleries, and vibrant festivals. Engage with the warm and welcoming locals who are proud of their heritage.

4. **Outdoor Adventures:** For those seeking adventure, Dubrovnik offers a range of activities, from hiking the surrounding hills and islands to kayaking along the city's walls. You can even take day trips to explore nearby islands and national parks.

5. **Mouthwatering Cuisine:** Croatian cuisine is a delightful mix of Mediterranean and Eastern European flavors. Taste local delicacies, savor fresh seafood, and indulge in traditional dishes that will delight your taste buds.

6. **Warm Mediterranean Climate:** Dubrovnik enjoys a Mediterranean climate with long, sunny summers. It's an ideal destination for sunseekers, beach lovers, and water enthusiasts.

Dubrovnik Old Town (Stari Grad)

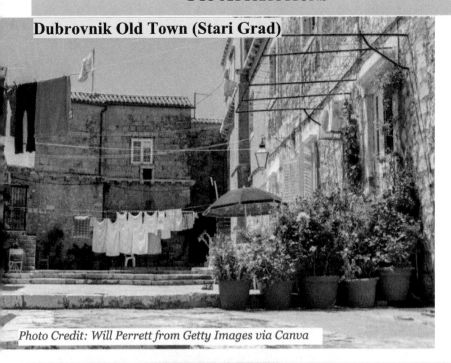

Photo Credit: Will Perrett from Getty Images via Canva

City Walls

Photo Credit: Cascoly/Canva

Lokrum Island

Photo Credit: Bepslabor/Canva

Fort Lovrijenac

Photo Credit: Rognar/Canva

Dubrovnik Cathedral

Photo Credit: Phant from Getty Images via Canva

Dubrovnik is a destination that promises a memorable experience throughout the year. However, proper planning is essential to ensure your trip aligns with your interests and preferences. This section of the guide will cover essential information to help you plan your visit.

When to Visit

Dubrovnik enjoys a Mediterranean climate, which means mild, wet winters and hot, dry summers. The best time to visit depends on your preferences:

- **Spring (April to June):** Spring is a fantastic time to visit if you prefer milder temperatures and fewer crowds. The flowers are in full bloom, and you can enjoy outdoor activities without the scorching summer heat.

- **Summer (July to August):** This is the high season when Dubrovnik sees the most visitors. It's the best time for beach lovers and water activities. However, it can get very crowded, and prices tend to be higher.

- **Autumn (September to October):** Early autumn is another excellent time to visit. The weather is still pleasant, and the crowds begin to thin out. You can enjoy the beauty of Dubrovnik without the peak-season rush.

- **Winter (November to March):** While it's the low season, some travelers enjoy the tranquility of Dubrovnik during the winter. The city is less crowded, and you can experience the local culture and festivals. Just be prepared for cooler, sometimes rainy weather.

Visa and Entry Requirements

Before traveling to Dubrovnik, make sure to check the visa and entry requirements based on your nationality. As of my last knowledge update in September 2021, Croatia is a member of the European

Union, and entry requirements may vary. Here are some general guidelines:

- **EU/EEA Citizens:** If you are a citizen of an EU/EEA country, you can enter Croatia with a valid ID card or passport, and no visa is required.

- **Non-EU/EEA Citizens:** Check with the Croatian embassy or consulate in your country for specific visa requirements. Typically, visitors from many countries can stay in Croatia for up to 90 days within a 180-day period for tourism purposes.

Currency and Money Matters

- **Currency:** The currency used in Croatia is the Croatian Kuna (HRK). While some places may accept euros, it's advisable to use the local currency for better exchange rates.

- **ATMs:** ATMs are widely available throughout Dubrovnik, including the Old Town. You can withdraw Kuna using your debit or credit card. Check with your bank regarding foreign transaction fees.

- **Credit Cards:** Credit and debit cards are widely accepted in hotels, restaurants, and shops. However, it's a good idea to carry some cash for small purchases and in case you visit more remote areas.

Language and Communication

- **Official Language:** The official language in Croatia is Croatian. However, in tourist areas like Dubrovnik, you'll find that many people working in the hospitality and service industry speak English, as well as other languages like German and Italian.

- **Communication:** To stay connected, consider purchasing a local SIM card or an international roaming plan for your mobile phone. Dubrovnik has good mobile network coverage.

Travel Insurance

Travel insurance is an essential part of your trip planning. It provides financial protection in case of unexpected events like trip cancellations, medical emergencies, or lost luggage. It's highly recommended to have comprehensive travel insurance before visiting Dubrovnik. Make sure to read the policy details and understand what it covers.

Dubrovnik is a well-connected city, and there are several ways to reach this beautiful destination.

Arriving by Air

Dubrovnik Airport (Čilipi Airport) is the primary gateway to the city. The airport is located approximately 15 kilometers south of Dubrovnik's Old Town. Here's what you need to know when arriving by air:

- **International Flights:** Dubrovnik Airport handles both domestic and international flights. Many major European cities have direct flights to Dubrovnik, making it convenient for international travelers.

- **Airport Transfers:** You can reach the city center from the airport by various means, including airport shuttles, taxis, and private transfers. The airport is well-connected to Dubrovnik's main bus station.

- **Car Rentals:** Car rental services are available at the airport, offering flexibility in exploring the surrounding areas.

Arriving by Land

If you're traveling to Dubrovnik by land, you have a few options:

- **Bus:** Dubrovnik is connected to neighboring cities and countries via an extensive bus network. You can take a bus from cities like Split, Zagreb, or even from nearby countries like Montenegro and Bosnia and Herzegovina.

- **Private Car:** If you're traveling from neighboring countries, you can drive to Dubrovnik. Ensure you have the necessary border-crossing documents and comply with local traffic rules.

Arriving by Sea

Dubrovnik's coastal location makes it accessible by sea, and it's a popular stop for cruise ships. Here's what to know about arriving by sea:

- **Cruise Ships:** Dubrovnik is a well-known port of call for numerous cruise lines. Passengers can easily disembark and explore the Old Town on foot.

- **Ferry Services:** You can also reach Dubrovnik by ferry from nearby islands like Korčula, Mljet, and the Elaphiti Islands. The Jadrolinija ferry company operates many of these routes.

Transportation within the City

Dubrovnik's Old Town is best explored on foot due to its compact size and pedestrian-friendly layout. However, for getting around the city and its surrounding areas, there are several transportation options:

- **City Buses:** Dubrovnik has a network of city buses that connect the Old Town with various neighborhoods and suburbs. Tickets can be purchased from the driver or at kiosks.

- **Taxis:** Taxis are readily available in the city. Ensure the taxi has a meter or agree on a fare before starting the journey.

- **Boats and Ferries:** You can take boats and ferries to explore nearby islands or simply enjoy a scenic boat ride. Popular destinations include Lokrum, the Elaphiti Islands, and other nearby coastal towns.

- **Car Rentals:** While a car is not necessary for exploring the Old Town, renting a car can be a great option if you want to visit more remote areas or take day trips. Ensure you are familiar with local driving rules and regulations.

Dubrovnik offers a wide range of accommodation options to suit all budgets and preferences. Whether you're looking for historical charm, stunning sea views, or modern amenities, you'll find the perfect place to stay.

Types of Accommodation

1. **Hotels:** Dubrovnik has a variety of hotels, from boutique establishments in the Old Town to larger, beachfront resorts. You can choose from budget-friendly options to luxurious five-star accommodations.

2. **Hostels:** If you're traveling on a tight budget, there are hostels both in the Old Town and outside of it, offering dormitory-style and private rooms.

3. **Apartments and Guesthouses:** Many locals rent out apartments and guesthouses, often located in historic buildings. This option is ideal for those seeking a more local experience and often includes kitchens for self-catering.

4. **Villas and Holiday Homes:** For a more private and upscale experience, you can rent a villa or holiday home in and around Dubrovnik, some with private pools and stunning views.

5. **Campsites:** If you're an outdoor enthusiast, Dubrovnik also offers campsites along the coast and on nearby islands.

Best Areas to Stay

1. **Old Town:** Staying within the city walls is an excellent choice if you want to be close to Dubrovnik's main attractions. You'll find charming boutique hotels and guesthouses here. Keep in mind that it can be more expensive and crowded.

2. **Ploče:** This neighborhood offers fantastic views of the Old Town and is still within walking distance. It's a great option if

you want to be close to the action but prefer a quieter atmosphere.

3. **Lapad:** Located to the west of the Old Town, Lapad offers a range of accommodations, beautiful beaches, and a more relaxed vibe.

4. **Gruž:** If you prefer a local, residential area, Gruž is a good choice. It's well-connected by public transportation and offers a variety of accommodation options.

5. **Babin Kuk:** This area includes the Babin Kuk Peninsula and the Lapad Peninsula. It's home to some of the city's best beach resorts and family-friendly hotels.

Budget, Mid-Range, and Luxury Options

1. **Budget:** Look for hostels, guesthouses, and apartments outside the Old Town for budget-friendly options. Lapad and Gruž offer affordable accommodations while still being conveniently located.

2. **Mid-Range:** In Lapad, you'll find mid-range hotels with excellent amenities. This area offers good value for your money and a more relaxed atmosphere.

3. **Luxury:** For a luxurious experience, consider staying within the Old Town at one of the historic hotels or opt for beachfront resorts in Babin Kuk. These upscale options offer top-notch service and amenities.

Booking Tips

- **Book in Advance:** During the high season, especially in summer, Dubrovnik can get very crowded, and accommodations tend to fill up quickly. It's advisable to book your accommodation well in advance, especially if you have specific preferences.

- **Consider Shoulder Seasons:** To avoid the peak-season crowds and get better deals on accommodations, consider visiting in the shoulder seasons of spring or early autumn.

- **Read Reviews:** Before booking, read reviews on websites like TripAdvisor, Booking.com, or Airbnb to ensure the accommodation meets your expectations.

- **Check Cancellation Policies:** Make sure to understand the cancellation policies of your chosen accommodation in case your plans change.

- **Local Agencies:** Consider using local rental agencies or contacting hosts directly if you're booking apartments or holiday homes. They can often provide more personalized assistance.

Recommended Accommodations

Budget Accommodation:

1. **Youth Hostel Dubrovnik**
   - Address: Petra Svačića 44, 20000 Dubrovnik
   - Estimated Cost: €20 - €50 per night
2. **Guesthouse And Rooms Lejletul**
   - Address: Petra Kresimira IV 30, 20000 Dubrovnik
   - Estimated Cost: €30 - €70 per night
3. **Rooms Vicelic**
   - Address: Plinarska 3, 20000 Dubrovnik
   - Estimated Cost: €40 - €80 per night
4. **Guesthouse Peter**
   - Address: Ul. Stjepana Radića 25, 20000 Dubrovnik
   - Estimated Cost: €50 - €100 per night

Mid-Range Accommodation:

1. **Hotel Lapad**
   - Address: Lapadska obala 37, 20000 Dubrovnik
   - Estimated Cost: €80 - €150 per night
2. **Guesthouse Lile**
   - Address: Put od Bosanke 10, 20000 Dubrovnik
   - Estimated Cost: €60 - €120 per night
3. **Hotel Kompas**
   - Address: Ul. kardinala Stepinca 21, 20000 Dubrovnik
   - Estimated Cost: €100 - €200 per night
4. **Hotel Adria**
   - Address: Radisson Blu Resort & Spa, Dubrovnik Sun Gardens, Na Moru 1, 20234, Orašac
   - Estimated Cost: €120 - €250 per night

Luxury Accommodation:
1. **Hotel Excelsior Dubrovnik**
   - Address: Frana Supila 12, 20000 Dubrovnik
   - Estimated Cost: €200 - €400+ per night
2. **Villa Orsula**
   - Address: Frana Supila 14, 20000 Dubrovnik
   - Estimated Cost: €250 - €500+ per night
3. **Hotel Bellevue Dubrovnik**
   - Address: Pera Čingrije 7, 20000 Dubrovnik
   - Estimated Cost: €250 - €500+ per night
4. **Villa Dubrovnik**
   - Address: Ul. Vlaha Bukovca 6, 20000 Dubrovnik
   - Estimated Cost: €400 - €800+ per night

Please note that these are estimated costs and can vary based on the time of year, room type, and special offers. It's advisable to check their websites for the most accurate and current pricing information.

Local Culture and Etiquette:

1. **Respect for Tradition:** Dubrovnik has a rich cultural heritage, so be respectful of local customs and traditions. Dress modestly when visiting churches and religious sites.

2. **Greetings:** A common way to greet someone is with a handshake and a friendly "Dobar dan" (Good day) or "Bok" (Hello). In tourist areas, English is widely spoken, but learning a few basic Croatian phrases can be appreciated by locals.

3. **Tipping:** Tipping is customary in restaurants, and a service charge may not be included in the bill. It's common to leave a tip of around 10-15% of the total bill.

4. **Punctuality:** Croatians value punctuality, so it's important to be on time for appointments and reservations.

5. **Public Displays of Affection:** While not frowned upon, it's best to keep public displays of affection moderate.

6. **Conservative Dress:** When visiting churches or religious sites, dress modestly with covered shoulders and knees.

Currency and Banking:

1. **Currency:** The official currency of Croatia is the Croatian Kuna (HRK). While some places may accept euros, it's advisable to use the local currency for better exchange rates.

2. **ATMs:** ATMs are widely available throughout Dubrovnik, including the Old Town. You can withdraw Kuna using your debit or credit card. Check with your bank regarding foreign transaction fees.

3. **Credit Cards:** Credit and debit cards are widely accepted in hotels, restaurants, and shops. Visa and MasterCard are the most commonly accepted. American Express and Diners Club are less commonly used.

4. **Currency Exchange:** You can exchange foreign currency at banks, exchange offices, and some hotels. It's recommended to use authorized exchange offices for fair rates.

Health and Safety:

1. **Travel Insurance:** Ensure you have comprehensive travel insurance that covers medical emergencies, trip cancellations, and lost luggage. Check if it covers activities such as hiking or water sports.

2. **Healthcare:** Medical facilities in Dubrovnik are generally of high quality. The European Health Insurance Card (EHIC) is valid in

SAFETY

Dubrovnik is a safe destination for travelers. Exercise common-sense safety precautions, such as safeguarding your belongings and avoiding poorly lit or deserted areas at night.

Emergency Numbers:

In case of emergencies, dial 112 for general emergency services or 194 for police.

Croatia, so European citizens can receive necessary healthcare at the same cost as locals.

3. **Natural Hazards:** Croatia experiences occasional earthquakes, so be aware of emergency procedures if you feel a strong tremor.

Local Laws and Regulations:

1. **Smoking:** Smoking is prohibited in indoor public spaces, including restaurants and bars. There are designated smoking areas.

2. **Alcohol Consumption:** The legal drinking age in Croatia is 18. Public drinking, especially in the Old Town, is discouraged and may be subject to fines.

3. **Littering:** Dispose of trash in designated bins. Littering is subject to fines.

4. **Photography:** Be respectful when taking photographs, especially of locals. Always ask for permission when photographing people.

5. **Bathing Attire:** It's important to wear appropriate swimwear at beaches and not walk around in bathing suits outside beach areas.

6. **Drug Laws:** Possession and use of illegal drugs are strictly prohibited in Croatia and can result in severe penalties.

EXPLORING DUBROVNIK

The Old Town

Photo Credit: R-J-Seymour/Canva

Photo Credit: RudyBalasko/Canva

OLD TOWN

- Dubrovnik's Old Town, often referred to as the "Pearl of the Adriatic," is a UNESCO World Heritage Site. It is one of the best-preserved medieval towns in Europe and a testament to the city's historical significance.

- Founded in the 7th century, the Old Town has withstood centuries of challenges, including earthquakes and conflicts, and continues to enchant visitors with its well-preserved architecture.

- The Old Town is enclosed by massive stone walls, which were built to protect the city from threats and can be explored today, offering panoramic views of the city and the Adriatic Sea.

- The city is known for its distinctive terracotta roofs, Baroque and Renaissance architecture, and charming streets. The Old Town is a pedestrian-only zone, making it perfect for leisurely strolls.

City Walls:

Photo Credit: Cascoly/Canva

- The Dubrovnik City Walls are an iconic feature of the Old Town. They encircle the city and provide breathtaking views of the Adriatic Sea and the Old Town's architecture.

- You can walk along the city walls, which stretch for about 1.2 miles (2 kilometers) and consist of several towers and fortifications. The walls offer a glimpse into the city's historical defenses, with narrow passages and hidden nooks.

- Don't forget to bring your camera, as the views from the walls are incredibly photogenic, especially during sunset.

- The City Walls are open to visitors year-round, but they can be quite crowded during the high tourist season, so consider visiting early in the morning or later in the day for a quieter experience.

Stradun (Placa):

Photo Credit: Leamus/Canva

- Stradun, also known as Placa, is the main street of the Old Town. It is a wide, limestone-paved pedestrian street lined with shops, restaurants, and historic buildings.

- Stradun runs from the Pile Gate (western entrance) to the Ploče Gate (eastern entrance), dividing the Old Town in half. It's the central artery of Dubrovnik and a perfect starting point for exploring the city.

- Along Stradun, you'll find many historical sites, such as the Sponza Palace, Rector's Palace, and the Church of St. Blaise, all showcasing Dubrovnik's architectural and cultural heritage.

- Stradun is a great place to enjoy a leisurely walk, do some shopping, or simply soak in the atmosphere of this remarkable city.

Historic Monuments
1. **Rector's Palace:**

This 16th-century palace served as the administrative center of the Republic of Ragusa (Dubrovnik). It's an excellent example of Gothic and Renaissance architecture and now houses the Cultural Historical Museum.

Photo Credit: Knežev dvor

2. Sponza Palace:

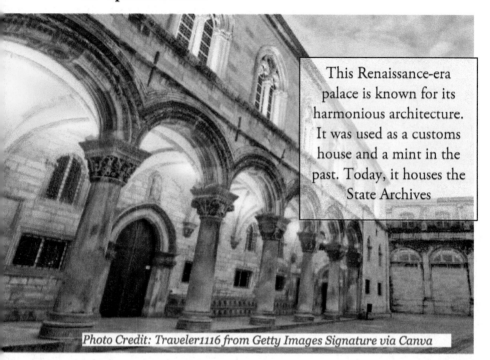

This Renaissance-era palace is known for its harmonious architecture. It was used as a customs house and a mint in the past. Today, it houses the State Archives

Photo Credit: Traveler1116 from Getty Images Signature via Canva

3. Church of St. Blaise:

This Baroque-style church, dedicated to the city's patron saint, St. Blaise, is a significant religious monument. It's known for its elegant design and a statue of the saint.

Photo Credit: Romanbabakin/Canva

4. Bell Tower:

Located near the Sponza Palace, this tower offers a great vantage point for views of the Old Town. The current tower was constructed after the original was destroyed in an earthquake.

Photo Credit: Dbvirago/Canva

5. Minčeta Tower:

Photo Credit: Spooh/Canva

Part of the city's defensive walls, Minčeta Tower is a prominent fortress with panoramic views of Dubrovnik. It's one of the city's most iconic defensive structures.

6. Onofrio's Fountain:

Built in the 15th century, this large fountain provided fresh water to the city and is a testament to the city's sophisticated water supply system.

Photo Credit: Jkraft5/Canva

7. Orlando's Column:

This stone column, crowned with a statue of the medieval knight Orlando, has stood in Dubrovnik's center for centuries. It symbolizes the city's independence and freedom.

Photo Credit: GoodLifeStudio from Getty Images Signature via Canva

1. **Dubrovnik Cathedral:**

Also known as the Cathedral of the Assumption of the Virgin Mary, this Baroque-style cathedral features an impressive interior and a treasury that houses religious artifacts and relics.

Photo Credit: Typhoonski via Canva

2. **Franciscan Monastery:**

Home to one of the oldest pharmacies in Europe, this 14th-century monastery boasts a stunning cloister and a rich collection of art and manuscripts.

Photo Credit: Kensorrie from Getty Images Signature via Canva

Museums and Galleries
Museums:

1. **Dubrovnik Museums:** The Dubrovnik Museums is a group of museums, including the Rector's Palace, the Maritime Museum, the Ethnographic Museum, and the Archaeological Museum. Each offers a unique perspective on Dubrovnik's history and culture.

2. **Cultural Historical Museum:** Located in the Rector's Palace, this museum showcases a diverse collection of art, artifacts, and historical exhibits. It offers insight into the city's medieval past.

3. **War Photo Limited:** This museum focuses on the impact of war through the lens of photography. It presents thought-provoking exhibits from conflict zones worldwide and highlights the importance of visual storytelling.

4. **Love Stories Museum:** A unique museum dedicated to love and relationships, it explores the many facets of love and features personal stories and artifacts.

5. **Dulčić-Masle-Pulitika Gallery:** This art gallery features contemporary and modern art from Croatian and international artists. It's a hub for artistic expression and creativity.

6. **Ruđer Bošković Institute:** A scientific research center with a museum that honors the life and work of Ruđer Bošković, an eminent physicist and astronomer from Dubrovnik.

7. **Museum of Modern Art Dubrovnik:** Located in a former Banac Mansion, this museum showcases a diverse collection of contemporary and modern art, including works by Croatian artists.

Galleries:

1. **Art Workshop Lazareti:** A creative hub for contemporary art and cultural events, it often hosts exhibitions, workshops, and performances.

2. **Art Gallery Dubrovnik:** Situated within the Dominican Monastery, this gallery features a collection of contemporary paintings, sculptures, and other forms of visual art.

3. **Art Studio Radoslav:** A gallery run by the artist Radoslav Putar, displaying his unique and colorful artwork inspired by Dubrovnik and the Mediterranean.

4. **Art Gallery Dulčić Masle Pulitika:** In addition to the museum, this gallery exhibits contemporary art by various local and international artists.

5. **Art Gallery Hadžiselimović:** Located in the heart of the Old Town, this gallery presents a selection of contemporary Croatian art, including paintings and sculptures.

6. **Art Pavilion Dubrovnik:** Situated in a charming park near the Old Town, this gallery hosts exhibitions by local and international artists.

Local Markets

1. **Gundulićeva Poljana Market (Dubrovnik Old Town Market):** Located in the heart of the Old Town, this bustling market offers a wide range of products. You can find fresh fruits, vegetables, local cheeses, honey, homemade wines, and a variety of traditional Croatian products. The market is open daily in the morning.

2. **Gruž Market:** Situated in the Gruž neighborhood, this open-air market is the largest in Dubrovnik. You can purchase a diverse selection of fruits, vegetables, seafood, and local

products. It's a great place to experience the daily life of locals and enjoy some delicious Croatian specialties.

3. **Green Market Lapad:** Located in the Lapad area, this market offers fresh produce, fish, and local products. It's an excellent option for those staying in the Lapad Peninsula, as it's within walking distance of many hotels and accommodations.

4. **Konavle Artisan Market:** If you're interested in unique, handmade souvenirs and local crafts, consider visiting the Konavle Artisan Market in the Konavle region, just outside Dubrovnik. You can find traditional textiles, pottery, and other handmade items created by local artisans.

5. **Sunday Open Market in Lapad:** Held every Sunday in Lapad, this market features a variety of items, from clothing and accessories to antiques. It's a fun place to explore and perhaps find some hidden gems.

6. **Cavtat Market:** If you plan to visit the charming town of Cavtat, you can explore its local market. It offers fresh produce, local crafts, and souvenirs in a beautiful coastal setting.

Beaches and Swimming Spots:

1. **Banje Beach:** Located near the Old Town, Banje Beach is one of the most popular spots for swimming and sunbathing. It offers beautiful views of the city walls and the island of Lokrum.

2. **Sveti Jakov Beach:** This picturesque pebble beach is situated in a secluded cove and provides a more tranquil atmosphere. The crystal-clear waters make it ideal for swimming.

3. **Copacabana Beach:** Located in the Lapad area, Copacabana Beach is known for its family-friendly environment and water sports. It features water slides, beach bars, and plenty of sun loungers.

4. **Lokrum Island:** Take a short boat trip to Lokrum Island, where you can find secluded swimming spots, including the Mrtvo More (Dead Sea) lake, which is a unique natural attraction.

5. **Cavtat Beaches:** If you venture to the town of Cavtat, you'll discover a range of beautiful beaches along its coastline, offering a more relaxed environment.

Hiking and Nature Trails:

1. **Mount Srđ:** For panoramic views of Dubrovnik and the Adriatic Sea, hike to the summit of Mount Srđ. You can take a cable car to the top or choose to hike the well-marked trails.

2. **Mljet National Park:** On the nearby island of Mljet, explore the national park's lush forests, pristine lakes, and hiking trails. It's a day trip from Dubrovnik.

3. **Konavle Valley:** The Konavle region, just outside Dubrovnik, is a fantastic place for hiking and exploring nature. Numerous

trails wind through picturesque landscapes and offer scenic views.

4. **Elafiti Islands:** Visit the Elafiti Islands, such as Lopud and Šipan, which offer pleasant hiking routes through olive groves and to old ruins.

Kayaking and Sailing:

1. **Sea Kayaking:** Explore Dubrovnik's coastline and the nearby Elafiti Islands by sea kayak. You can join guided tours that take you to hidden caves and secluded beaches.

2. **Sailing:** Dubrovnik is a sailing paradise, and you can charter a boat to explore the crystal-clear waters of the Adriatic. There are various sailing excursions and boat tours available.

3. **Diving:** Discover the underwater world of Dubrovnik by going scuba diving. Several dive centers offer trips to dive sites with vibrant marine life and shipwrecks.

4. **Snorkeling:** Snorkeling is a popular activity along Dubrovnik's coastline. You can rent or bring your own snorkeling equipment and explore the vibrant underwater world.

Day Trips to Nearby Islands

1. **Lokrum Island:** Lokrum is the closest island to Dubrovnik and can be reached by a short boat ride. It's a nature lover's paradise with lush botanical gardens, peacocks, and walking trails. The island also has a historic monastery and a beautiful saltwater lake known as the Mrtvo More or the Dead Sea.

2. **Elafiti Islands:** The Elafiti archipelago, consisting of several islands, is known for its pristine nature and crystal-clear waters. The main islands to consider for day trips are Lopud, Šipan, and Koločep. Each island offers a unique experience, including sandy beaches, historic sites, and charming villages.

3. **Mljet Island:** Mljet is one of the largest islands in the Adriatic and is known for its stunning Mljet National Park. The park features two saltwater lakes, Veliko and Malo Jezero, where you can swim, kayak, and explore a small island with a 12th-century Benedictine monastery.

4. **Korčula Island:** Korčula is known for its medieval Old Town, said to be the birthplace of the famous explorer Marco Polo. The island boasts historic architecture, charming streets, and beautiful beaches. The town of Korčula itself is a popular destination for day trips.

5. **Šipan Island:** The island of Šipan is part of the Elafiti archipelago and is particularly peaceful. It's known for its beautiful landscapes, vineyards, and the ruins of the Skočibuha Castle. You can explore the island on foot or by renting a bike.

6. **Cavtat:** While not an island, the town of Cavtat is located on the southernmost tip of the Croatian coastline, and it's a popular day trip destination from Dubrovnik. Cavtat offers a picturesque harbor, historic architecture, and lovely promenades.

7. **Badija Island:** Located near the town of Korčula, Badija is a small, tranquil island with a Franciscan monastery, beautiful beaches, and opportunities for hiking and swimming.

Dubrovnik's Cuisine:

1. **Seafood:** Given its coastal location, seafood is a staple of Dubrovnik's cuisine. Fresh fish, shrimp, mussels, and squid are commonly used in various dishes.

2. **Olive Oil:** High-quality olive oil is essential in Dubrovnik's cuisine, both for cooking and as a condiment.

3. **Wine:** The region surrounding Dubrovnik, known as Konavle, is famous for its vineyards. Local wines, such as Plavac Mali and Posip, complement the cuisine perfectly.

4. **Herbs and Spices:** Herbs like rosemary, basil, and sage, as well as spices such as garlic and bay leaves, are frequently used to season dishes.

5. **Fresh Produce:** Fruits and vegetables like figs, grapes, tomatoes, and bell peppers are commonly used in local dishes.

6. **Grilled Meats:** While seafood takes center stage, you'll also find grilled meats like lamb and pork prepared with Mediterranean flavors.

7. **Local Cheese:** Dubrovnik produces delicious cheese, including sheep's milk cheese and soft, creamy varieties.

Local Food and Culinary Traditions:

1. Peka:

Peka is a traditional method of cooking, where meat or seafood is slow-cooked under an iron bell, often with potatoes and vegetables. This method infuses dishes with rich, smoky flavors.

2. Octopus Salad:

Photo Credit: Kajakiki/Canva

Octopus salad, a popular appetizer, features tender pieces of octopus mixed with vegetables, olive oil, and herbs.

3. Black Risotto (Crni Rižot):

Photo Credit: Zeleno/Canva

This dish gets its dark color from squid ink and is a unique and flavorful specialty in Dubrovnik. It's often served with fresh seafood.

4. Rozata:

Photo Credit: Peter TG

A Dubrovnik dessert, rozata is a custard pudding with a caramelized sugar topping, similar to crème caramel.

5. Buzara:

Buzara is a flavorful seafood stew made with garlic, white wine, and tomatoes. It's typically served with fresh bread to soak up the delicious sauce.

Must-Try Dishes:

1. **Dalmatian Brodet:** A fisherman's stew made with a variety of seafood, tomatoes, and Mediterranean herbs. It's a hearty and flavorful dish.

2. **Ston Oysters:** The town of Ston, near Dubrovnik, is famous for its oyster beds. Try fresh oysters with a squeeze of lemon for a true taste of the sea.

3. **Lamb Under the Bell (Janjetina ispod peke):** This is a delicious dish of tender lamb roasted with herbs and potatoes under a bell-like cover.

4. **Squid Stuffed with Prosciutto and Cheese:** A delectable dish featuring squid stuffed with prosciutto, cheese, and herbs, then grilled to perfection.

5. **Skampi na Buzaru:** A delightful dish of prawns or scampi prepared in the buzara style, with garlic, white wine, and tomatoes.

6. **Pasticada:** While not native to Dubrovnik, pasticada is a Croatian classic. It's a slow-cooked beef dish, usually served with gnocchi, and is full of rich flavors.

7. **Rakija:** This is a popular Croatian brandy made from various fruits, and it's often offered as a digestive after a meal.

Popular Restaurants and Cafes:

1. **Nautika Restaurant:** Located just outside the city walls with a stunning view of the Adriatic, Nautika is known for its fine dining and creative seafood dishes. It's a top choice for a special occasion.

2. **Proto:** Situated on a charming street in the Old Town, Proto is one of the city's oldest restaurants. It offers traditional Dalmatian cuisine with a modern twist.

3. **Restaurant 360:** Perched on the city walls, this restaurant provides breathtaking panoramic views of the Old Town and the sea. It offers a diverse menu with an emphasis on seafood.

4. **Taj Mahal Dubrovnik:** For a change of flavor, try Taj Mahal, offering authentic Bosnian and Middle Eastern dishes, such as cevapi and pita bread.

5. **Horizont:** Located in Lapad, Horizont offers a wide range of Mediterranean and international dishes. It's known for its seafood and has a pleasant terrace overlooking the sea.

6. **Arsenal Taverna:** Situated in the heart of the Old Town, this charming tavern serves traditional Croatian dishes in a historic setting.

7. **Dubravka 1836:** Overlooking the Old Town's walls and the sea, Dubravka 1836 offers a combination of international and Croatian cuisine, including fresh seafood and pasta.

8. **Lady Pi-Pi:** A cozy and popular spot for grilled meats and seafood, with a lovely terrace and a picturesque view of the Old Town.

9. **Café Buža:** Tucked away in the cliffs outside the city walls, Café Buža is an unforgettable spot for a drink with a view. It's a perfect place to enjoy a casual drink while watching the sunset.

Dining Etiquette:
1. **Reservations:** It's advisable to make reservations, especially at popular restaurants, to secure a table, particularly during the tourist season.

2. **Tipping:** Tipping is customary in Croatia, and a 10-15% tip is appreciated for good service. However, check the bill as some restaurants include a service charge.

3. **Paying the Bill:** In Croatia, it's typical for the waiter to bring the bill to your table. You can pay directly at the table rather than at a cashier.

4. **Dress Code:** While Dubrovnik is generally relaxed, some upscale restaurants may have a dress code. For casual dining, resort wear is fine, but bring something slightly more formal for upscale restaurants.

5. **Splitting the Bill:** Splitting the bill is common, and most restaurants are accommodating when it comes to separate checks.

6. **Water and Bread:** It's common for restaurants to charge for water and bread, so confirm if these are complimentary or if there's an additional cost.

7. **Ordering Seafood:** When ordering seafood, you may be presented with the catch of the day for your selection. Ask about the preparation options, such as grilling or in a buzara sauce.

8. **Use of Cutlery:** The continental European style of eating is used, where the fork is held in the left hand and the knife in the right. In casual settings, the American style is also acceptable.

Bars and Pubs:

1. **Buža Bar:** This unique bar is carved into the cliffs outside the city walls and offers stunning views of the sea. It's a great spot for sunset cocktails.

2. **Banje Beach Bar:** Located on Banje Beach, this bar is known for its trendy atmosphere, DJ sets, and cocktails. It's a lively place both day and night.

3. **D'Vino Wine Bar:** For wine enthusiasts, D'Vino Wine Bar is a cozy spot to sample a wide selection of Croatian wines in the Old Town.

4. **Irish Pub Gaffe:** If you're in the mood for a traditional pub experience, head to Gaffe for a wide range of beers and a friendly atmosphere.

5. **Troubadour Jazz Cafe:** Enjoy live jazz performances in a charming Old Town location, often featuring local and international artists.

6. **Karaka Bar:** Located on a historic ship, the Karaka Bar offers a unique setting for enjoying cocktails while overlooking the Old Town.

7. **Hemingway Bar:** Named after the famous author who spent time in Dubrovnik, this bar is known for its creative cocktails and a relaxed ambiance.

Clubs and Nightlife Hotspots:

1. **Revelin Club:** One of Dubrovnik's top clubs, Revelin is situated in a 16th-century fortress. It hosts international DJs and a range of music genres, making it a vibrant nightlife hotspot.

2. **Culture Club Revelin:** Located next to Revelin Club, this venue often hosts live concerts and events in addition to club nights.

3. **EastWest Beach Club:** With a beachfront location, this club offers beach parties, DJ sets, and a lively atmosphere. It's a popular summer destination.

4. **Copacabana Beach Club:** Located on Copacabana Beach in Lapad, this beach club hosts daytime parties and DJ events with a view of the Adriatic Sea.

5. **Taverna Otto:** A bar and club, Taverna Otto is known for its diverse music selection and dance parties. It's a favorite among locals and tourists alike.

6. **Republika Club:** Situated in the Lapad area, Republika Club offers a more intimate nightlife experience with various music styles and a pleasant outdoor terrace.

7. **Fuego Club:** This club is a hot spot for Latin and reggaeton music, offering a vibrant atmosphere and dance floor.

8. **La Bodega Night Bar:** Located in the heart of the Old Town, this bar transforms into a vibrant nightlife destination after sunset.

Live Music Venues:

1. **Rooftop Bars:** Many rooftop bars in Dubrovnik offer live music performances, particularly during the summer months. Enjoy live jazz, acoustic, or traditional Croatian music while taking in stunning views of the city.

2. **Troubadour Jazz Cafe:** This intimate jazz cafe in the Old Town often hosts live jazz performances featuring local and international musicians. It's a great place to unwind with some smooth tunes.

3. **Park Orsula:** Located in a park with panoramic views of Dubrovnik, Park Orsula is a unique outdoor venue that hosts various cultural events, including live music concerts.

4. **Old Town Street Performers:** As you wander through the Old Town, you may come across street performers playing traditional Croatian music or classical instruments. These impromptu performances add to the city's charm.

Cultural Performances:

1. **Dubrovnik Summer Festival:** This renowned festival, held from mid-July to mid-August, is one of the highlights of the cultural calendar. It features a wide range of performances, including theater, opera, dance, and classical music, in various historic venues throughout the city.

2. **Lindjo Folklore Ensemble:** Lindjo is a traditional Croatian folklore ensemble that performs lively dances and songs. You can often catch their performances in the Old Town.

3. **Dubrovnik Symphony Orchestra:** Enjoy classical music concerts by the Dubrovnik Symphony Orchestra, which performs in various locations, including the Rector's Palace and the Sponza Palace.

4. **Open-Air Cinema:** During the summer, open-air cinemas are set up in various locations in Dubrovnik, often screening classic films and providing a unique cultural experience.

5. **Medieval and Renaissance Performances:** Various theaters and cultural organizations in Dubrovnik occasionally host medieval and Renaissance-themed performances, including historical reenactments and theater productions.

Best Shopping Districts:
1. **Stradun (Placa):** The main street of the Old Town, Stradun, is lined with shops and boutiques. Here, you can find a range of items, from clothing and accessories to jewelry and local products. It's a great place for souvenir shopping.

2. **Old Town Boutiques:** Wander through the charming streets of the Old Town, and you'll discover numerous boutiques selling clothing, jewelry, ceramics, and artwork, often with a local touch.

3. **Gundulićeva Poljana Market:** Located in the heart of the Old Town, this daily market is the place to go for fresh produce, local products, and souvenirs, including lavender products, olive oil, and traditional sweets.

4. **Lapad and Gruž:** The Lapad and Gruž neighborhoods offer shopping opportunities in a more relaxed and less touristy environment. You can find a variety of shops, including clothing stores and supermarkets.

5. **Shopping Malls:** While there aren't large shopping malls within the Old Town, the suburbs of Dubrovnik have modern shopping centers like Mercante and Sub City, where you can find international and local brands.

Souvenirs and Unique Gifts:
1. **Lavender Products:** Lavender is a symbol of the region, and you can find a range of lavender-based products, including oils, soaps, sachets, and more.

2. **Ceramics:** Dubrovnik is known for its unique blue-and-white ceramics, often featuring intricate patterns and designs. These make for beautiful and authentic souvenirs.

3. **Traditional Croatian Embroidery:** Look for tablecloths, napkins, and clothing adorned with intricate Croatian embroidery, which is a cherished local craft.

4. **Local Artwork:** Dubrovnik is home to many talented artists. Explore local art galleries to find paintings, sculptures, and other forms of artwork to bring home as a special memento.

5. **Konavle Embroidery:** The Konavle region near Dubrovnik is known for its distinct embroidery styles. Look for handmade Konavle embroidery items, including traditional costumes and home decor.

6. **Olive Oil and Local Food:** High-quality olive oil is a sought-after souvenir, along with local cheeses, wines, and other food products.

7. **Dubrovnik Jewelry:** Many jewelry shops in the Old Town offer pieces inspired by the city's history and culture, often featuring nautical motifs and semi-precious stones.

8. **Traditional Instruments:** Croatian music has a rich tradition, and you can find traditional musical instruments like the tamburica (a type of lute) and the diple (a type of bagpipe) in select shops.

9. **Croatian Wine:** Croatia has a growing reputation for producing excellent wines. Consider buying a bottle or two of local wine to enjoy back home.

Elaphiti Islands:

Photo Credit: Goran Safarek from Getty Images via Canva

The Elaphiti Islands are a small archipelago off the coast of Dubrovnik, known for their natural beauty and peaceful ambiance. You can take a day trip to visit some of the islands:

- **Lopud:** Known for its sandy beaches and car-free environment, Lopud is a popular destination for a day of swimming and relaxation.

- **Šipan:** The largest of the Elaphiti Islands, Šipan offers scenic landscapes, olive groves, and charming fishing villages.

- **Koločep:** This tiny island features crystal-clear waters, hiking trails, and a lovely botanical garden.

- **Boat Tours:** Various boat tours and ferries depart from Dubrovnik to the Elaphiti Islands, allowing you to explore multiple islands in a single day.

Montenegro:

Photo Credit: Sorincolac/Canva

A day trip to Montenegro offers a chance to explore the stunning Bay of Kotor and experience a different culture:

- **Kotor:** Visit the UNESCO-listed town of Kotor, surrounded by dramatic mountain landscapes. Explore the Old Town, walk the city walls, and enjoy the local cuisine.

- **Perast:** A charming town on the bay, Perast is known for its baroque architecture and the beautiful islets of Our Lady of the Rocks and St. George.

- **Budva:** This coastal town boasts beautiful beaches, a historic Old Town, and a vibrant nightlife scene.

- **Bay of Kotor Boat Tour:** Consider taking a boat tour of the Bay of Kotor to enjoy the stunning views and visit various towns along the way.

Lokrum Island:

Photo Credit: Rognar/Canva

Lokrum Island is a short boat ride from Dubrovnik and is a delightful destination for a day trip:

- **Nature:** Explore the lush botanical gardens, hike the island's trails, and visit the ruins of a Benedictine monastery.

- **Swimming:** Lokrum offers several swimming spots along its rocky coast. The Dead Sea, a saltwater lake on the island, is also a popular place to swim.

- **Peacocks:** The island is home to a large peacock population, making for an interesting and picturesque sight.

- **Ferries:** Ferries to Lokrum Island depart regularly from Dubrovnik's Old Town port.

Other Nearby Attractions

1. Ston: Located about an hour's drive from Dubrovnik, Ston is known for its impressive medieval city walls, which are the second-longest preserved fortifications in the world. The town is also famous for its salt pans and delicious seafood.

2. Trsteno Arboretum: This historic Renaissance garden, situated about 20 kilometers from Dubrovnik, is the oldest arboretum in this part of the world. It features a variety of exotic plants, ornate fountains, and a tranquil atmosphere.

3. Konavle Valley: Located just south of Dubrovnik, the Konavle Valley is a picturesque rural area known for its scenic landscapes, traditional villages, and agritourism. You can visit local farms, taste traditional cuisine, and explore the charming countryside.

4. Cavtat: A beautiful coastal town located about 20 kilometers south of Dubrovnik, Cavtat is known for its historical sites, picturesque harbor, and lovely beaches. It's a great place to spend a relaxed day exploring.

5. Mljet National Park: While Mljet Island is a day trip in itself, you can also visit the Mljet National Park on the western end of the island. The park features two saltwater lakes, lush forests, and a small islet with a Benedictine monastery.

6. Mostar (Bosnia and Herzegovina): While it's a bit farther from Dubrovnik (about a 2.5-hour drive), Mostar is worth considering for a day trip. It's known for its iconic Stari Most (Old Bridge), Ottoman architecture, and vibrant marketplaces.

7. Pelješac Peninsula: This peninsula is known for its vineyards, especially those producing Dingač and Postup wines. You can explore the wineries, taste local wines, and enjoy the scenic beauty of the area.

8. Elaphiti Islands Extended Trip: While mentioned earlier, consider an extended visit to explore more of the Elaphiti Islands, including Lopud, Šipan, and Koločep, to experience their individual charm.

9. Dubrovnik Riviera Beaches: Many beautiful beaches and coves are located along the Dubrovnik Riviera, offering an ideal setting for a day of sunbathing and swimming.

3 Days in Dubrovnik: A Perfect Weekend Getaway

Day 1: Arrival and Old Town Exploration

- **Morning: Arrival in Dubrovnik**

    - Arrive at Dubrovnik Airport or the main bus station.

    - Check in to your accommodation.

- **Afternoon: Explore the Old Town**

    - Begin your visit in the historic Old Town. Walk through Pile Gate and start your exploration of this UNESCO World Heritage Site.

    - Visit the Onofrio's Fountain, the Franciscan Monastery, and the Rector's Palace.

    - Stroll along the Stradun (Placa), the city's main thoroughfare, and admire the architecture and atmosphere.

- **Evening: Dinner in the Old Town**

    - Choose one of the restaurants or taverns in the Old Town to savor your first Croatian meal. Try local seafood or traditional Croatian dishes.

    - After dinner, take a leisurely evening walk along the city walls for beautiful views of the illuminated Old Town.

Day 2: Dubrovnik City Walls and Island Escape

- **Morning: Dubrovnik City Walls**

    - Start your day with a visit to the city walls. Early morning is the best time to avoid the crowds and the heat.

    - Enjoy panoramic views of the Old Town and the Adriatic Sea.

- **Lunch: Old Town or Harbor**

    - Choose a café or restaurant in the Old Town for lunch or head to the harbor for a seafood meal.

- **Afternoon: Lokrum Island**

    - Take a short ferry ride to Lokrum Island.

    - Explore the lush gardens, visit the botanical garden, and swim in the saltwater lake.

    - Enjoy the peacocks that roam the island.

- **Evening: Sunset and Dinner**

    - Return to the Old Town for a relaxing evening.

    - As the sun sets, head to a popular spot like Buža Bar, where you can sip cocktails and enjoy the breathtaking view.

Day 3: Day Trip to Montenegro

- **Morning: Bay of Kotor, Montenegro**

  - Take a day trip to Montenegro and visit the stunning Bay of Kotor.

  - Explore the charming towns of Kotor and Perast, and maybe climb the city walls of Kotor for panoramic views.

- **Lunch: Montenegrin Cuisine**

  - Savor Montenegrin dishes at a local restaurant in Kotor or Perast.

- **Afternoon: Return to Dubrovnik**

  - Return to Dubrovnik in the late afternoon.

- **Evening: Farewell Dinner**

  - Enjoy a farewell dinner at a seafood restaurant in the Old Town or Lapad.

1-Week Adventure in Dubrovnik

Day 1: Arrival and Old Town Exploration

- **Morning: Arrival in Dubrovnik**

    - Arrive at Dubrovnik Airport or the main bus station.

    - Check in to your accommodation.

- **Afternoon: Explore the Old Town**

    - Begin your visit in the historic Old Town. Walk through Pile Gate and start your exploration of this UNESCO World Heritage Site.

    - Visit key landmarks, including the Onofrio's Fountain, the Franciscan Monastery, the Rector's Palace, and the Sponza Palace.

    - Stroll along the Stradun and enjoy the atmosphere.

- **Evening: Dinner in the Old Town**

    - Choose a restaurant in the Old Town to enjoy your first Croatian meal. Try local seafood or traditional dishes.

Day 2: Dubrovnik City Walls and Old Town

- **Morning: Dubrovnik City Walls**

    - Start your day by walking the city walls for the best views of the Old Town.

    - Take your time to admire the panoramic vistas.

- **Lunch: Old Town or Harbor**

    - Enjoy lunch in a charming café or restaurant in the Old Town or at the harbor.

- **Afternoon: Old Town Exploration**

    - Continue exploring the Old Town with visits to museums and churches, such as the Dubrovnik Cathedral and the Church of St. Blaise.

    - If you're interested in art, explore local galleries.

- **Evening: Sunset Cruise**

    - Take a sunset cruise to appreciate the city from the sea.

Day 3: Elaphiti Islands

- **Full-Day Elaphiti Islands Tour**

    - Take a day trip to the Elaphiti Islands. Explore Lopud, Šipan, and Koločep.

    - Enjoy swimming, sunbathing, and a leisurely lunch on one of the islands.

Day 4: Montenegro Day Trip

- **Full-Day Trip to Montenegro**

    - Visit the Bay of Kotor and the picturesque towns of Kotor and Perast.

    - Explore Kotor's Old Town and climb its city walls for stunning views.

    - Savor Montenegrin cuisine during lunch.

Day 5: Dubrovnik's Culinary Delights

- **Morning: Cooking Class**

    - Participate in a cooking class to learn how to prepare traditional Croatian dishes.

- **Afternoon: Wine Tasting**

    - Visit a local winery to taste Croatian wines and enjoy a relaxing afternoon surrounded by vineyards.

- **Evening: Dinner in Lapad**

    - Enjoy dinner in Lapad, known for its waterfront restaurants and diverse cuisine.

Day 6: Adventure and Nature

- **Morning: Kayaking**

    - Embark on a kayaking adventure, exploring the picturesque coastline and hidden coves.

- **Lunch: Beachside**

    - Have lunch at a beachfront restaurant to relax and enjoy the sea.

- **Afternoon: Srd Hill Hike**

    - Hike up Srd Hill to take in panoramic views of Dubrovnik and the surrounding area.

- **Evening: Farewell Dinner**

    - Savor a farewell dinner at a restaurant with sea views in the Old Town.

Day 7: Day of Leisure or Additional Day Trip

- **Leisure Day:** Spend the day at your own pace, perhaps returning to your favorite spots in the Old Town, shopping, or simply relaxing on the beach.

- **Additional Day Trip:** Alternatively, you can opt for another day trip to nearby destinations, such as Lokrum Island, Ston, or the Pelješac Peninsula.

Family-Friendly Itinerary

Day 1: Arrival and Settling In

- **Morning: Arrival in Dubrovnik**

    - Arrive at Dubrovnik Airport or the main bus station.

    - Check in to your family-friendly accommodation.

- **Afternoon: Relaxation and Orientation**

    - Spend the afternoon settling in, exploring your accommodation, and getting oriented in the local area.

- **Evening: Dinner in the Old Town**

    - Choose a family-friendly restaurant in the Old Town for your first meal in Dubrovnik.

Day 2: Old Town Exploration

- **Morning: Dubrovnik Old Town**

    - Begin your family adventure with a visit to the Old Town.

    - Explore key landmarks like the city walls, Stradun, and Onofrio's Fountain.

- **Lunch: Old Town**

    - Enjoy a family lunch in one of the charming Old Town restaurants.

- **Afternoon: Dubrovnik Aquarium and Maritimo Museum**
  - Visit the Dubrovnik Aquarium and Maritimo Museum, where kids can learn about marine life and maritime history.

- **Evening: Sunset Walk**
  - Take a leisurely walk in the Old Town in the evening and enjoy the sunset views.

Day 3: Island Excursion

- **Full-Day Trip to Lokrum Island**
  - Take a short ferry ride to Lokrum Island, a great place for kids with its botanical garden and peacocks.
  - Enjoy swimming in the saltwater lake and exploring the island.

Day 4: Family Adventure and Nature

- **Morning: Dubrovnik Cable Car**
  - Take the cable car to Srd Hill for breathtaking views of Dubrovnik and its surroundings.
  - Let the kids enjoy the panoramic views.

- **Lunch: Panoramic Restaurant**
  - Have lunch at the panoramic restaurant on Srd Hill, offering stunning vistas.

- **Afternoon: Sun Gardens Dubrovnik Resort**
    - Spend the afternoon at the Sun Gardens Dubrovnik Resort, where you can access the beach and swimming pools.

- **Evening: Dinner in Lapad**
    - Enjoy dinner at one of the family-friendly restaurants in Lapad.

Day 5: Island Adventures

- **Full-Day Trip to Elaphiti Islands**
    - Explore the Elaphiti Islands on a day trip, with opportunities for swimming, snorkeling, and exploring the islands' charm.

Day 6: Nature and Adventure

- **Morning: Sea Kayaking**
    - Embark on a family sea kayaking adventure along the Dubrovnik coastline.

- **Lunch: Beach Picnic**
    - Have a picnic lunch on one of the quiet beaches along the way.

- **Afternoon: Copacabana Beach**
    - Spend the afternoon at Copacabana Beach in Lapad, where kids can enjoy the waterslides and paddleboats.

- **Evening: Farewell Dinner**
  - Savor a farewell family dinner at a kid-friendly restaurant.

Day 7: Leisure and Souvenirs

- **Morning: Free Time**
  - Spend the morning at your own pace. You can relax on the beach, shop for souvenirs, or revisit your favorite places.

- **Lunch: Old Town**
  - Enjoy lunch in the Old Town at one of the family-friendly eateries.

- **Afternoon: Souvenir Shopping**
  - Allow the kids to pick out their favorite Dubrovnik souvenirs and enjoy an afternoon of shopping.

- **Evening: Farewell and Departure**

Budget Traveler's Guide

Day 1: Arrival and Old Town Orientation

- **Morning: Arrival in Dubrovnik**

    - Arrive at Dubrovnik Airport or the main bus station.

    - Use public transportation to reach your budget-friendly accommodation.

- **Afternoon: Explore the Old Town**

    - Begin your visit by walking through the Pile Gate into the Old Town.

    - Take a free self-guided walking tour to explore key landmarks, including the city walls and Onofrio's Fountain.

- **Evening: Affordable Dinner**

    - Choose a local konoba or tavern in the Old Town for an affordable dinner. Sample traditional Croatian dishes.

Day 2: Old Town Exploration

- **Morning: City Walls and Landmarks**

    - Invest in a City Walls ticket for stunning views. Start early to avoid crowds and the midday heat.

    - Visit free landmarks like the Franciscan Monastery and Rector's Palace.

- **Lunch: Local Eateries**

  - Look for local pizzerias or fast-food stands for a budget-friendly lunch.

- **Afternoon: Free Attractions**

  - Visit free attractions like Dubrovnik's Old Harbor and local parks.

- **Evening: Sunset Views**

  - Enjoy sunset views from public spots like the Buža Bar, where you can order a drink and admire the city.

Day 3: Island Escape on a Budget

- **Morning: Affordable Breakfast**

  - Grab a budget breakfast at a local bakery or café.

- **Full-Day Trip to Lokrum Island**

  - Take a budget-friendly ferry to Lokrum Island. Explore its lush gardens, enjoy the saltwater lake, and meet the peacocks.

- **Evening: Cheap Eats**

  - Return to Dubrovnik and look for affordable dining options like fast-food stalls or casual pizzerias.

Day 4: Day Trip to Montenegro

- **Full-Day Trip to Montenegro**

    - Take a budget-friendly group tour to Montenegro. Visit Kotor and Perast, and enjoy local cuisine.

Day 5: Hidden Gems and Budget Eats

- **Morning: Off-the-Beaten-Path**

    - Explore local neighborhoods and discover hidden gems such as churches and parks.

- **Lunch: Local Markets**

    - Opt for lunch at the local Gundulićeva Poljana Market, where you can find budget-friendly street food and snacks.

- **Afternoon: Sun Gardens Dubrovnik**

    - Spend the afternoon at the Sun Gardens Dubrovnik Resort, which offers budget-friendly access to the beach and swimming pools.

- **Evening: Dinner in Lapad**

    - Dine at affordable eateries in Lapad.

Day 6: Adventure and Nature on a Budget

- **Morning: Affordable Breakfast**
  - Enjoy breakfast at a local café or bakery in Lapad.
- **Sea Kayaking on a Budget**
  - Look for budget-friendly group sea kayaking tours to explore the coast.
- **Evening: Farewell Dinner**
  - Have a budget-friendly farewell dinner at a local tavern.

Day 7: Souvenirs and Farewell

- **Morning: Souvenir Shopping**
  - Spend the morning shopping for budget-friendly souvenirs and gifts.
- **Lunch: Picnic by the Sea**
  - Create a budget-friendly picnic and enjoy it by the sea.
- **Afternoon: Free Time**
  - Relax on the beach or explore more of Dubrovnik on a budget.
- **Evening: Farewell and Departure**

MAPS AND PRACTICAL RESOURCES

Tourist Map:

https://ontheworldmap.com/croatia/city/dubrovnik/dubrovnik-tourist-map.jpg

Sightseeing:

https://ontheworldmap.com/croatia/city/dubrovnik/dubrovnik-sightseeing-map.jpg

Attractions

1. **Dubrovnik Old Town (Stari Grad):** The heart of Dubrovnik is its historic Old Town. Walk through the city walls and explore the charming streets, squares, and historic buildings.

2. **City Walls:** Climb the city walls for breathtaking panoramic views of Dubrovnik, the Adriatic Sea, and the surrounding area.

3. **Lokrum Island:** A short ferry ride away, Lokrum Island offers lush gardens, a saltwater lake, and peacocks roaming freely.

4. **Fort Lovrijenac:** Perched on a cliff outside the city walls, Fort Lovrijenac provides great views of the Old Town and the sea. It's also famous for being featured in Game of Thrones.

5. **Dubrovnik Cathedral:** The Dubrovnik Cathedral is a beautiful Baroque-style church housing the Treasury, which includes religious relics and art.

6. **Rector's Palace:** Explore the Rector's Palace, a historic building that once served as the seat of the Republic of Ragusa.

7. **Franciscan Monastery:** Visit the Franciscan Monastery and its ancient pharmacy, one of the oldest in Europe.

8. **Onofrio's Fountain:** This monumental fountain, built in the 15th century, once supplied the city with fresh water.

9. **Buža Bar:** Enjoy a drink with stunning views on the cliffs overlooking the Adriatic Sea.

10. **Gundulićeva Poljana Market:** Located in the heart of the Old Town, this daily market offers fresh produce, local products, and souvenirs.

11. **Dubrovnik Aquarium and Maritimo Museum:** Learn about marine life and maritime history in this educational attraction.

12. **Srd Hill:** Hike up Srd Hill for breathtaking panoramic views of Dubrovnik and the surrounding area.

13. **Elaphiti Islands:** Take a day trip to the Elaphiti Islands, known for their natural beauty and peaceful ambiance.

14. **Dubrovnik Harbor:** Explore the Old Harbor with its boats, historic ships, and waterfront restaurants.

15. **Minceta Tower:** Part of the city walls, Minceta Tower offers impressive views and is one of the strongest fortresses in Dubrovnik.

16. **War Photo Limited:** This museum showcases powerful photography depicting the impact of war on the region.

17. **Sun Gardens Dubrovnik Resort:** Enjoy the beach, swimming pools, and other amenities at this coastal resort.

18. **Korčula Island:** Take a day trip to Korčula Island, known for its charming Old Town, traditional architecture, and local wine.

19. **Lapad Bay:** Relax on the beaches of Lapad Bay and explore the nearby promenade.

20. **Trsteno Arboretum:** Visit the historic Renaissance garden, known for its lush plants and elegant fountains.

Public Transportation Maps

Public transportation in Dubrovnik primarily consists of buses, as the city does not have a metro or tram system. The local bus service, run by Libertas Dubrovnik, is an efficient and affordable way to get around the city and its surroundings.

1. **Bus Network:** The bus network in Dubrovnik is extensive, covering the city itself as well as nearby neighborhoods and suburbs. Buses connect various parts of the city, including the Old Town (often referred to as "Gradske Zidine" or "Pile"), Lapad, Gruž, and Babin Kuk.

2. **Bus Fares:** You can purchase bus tickets from the bus drivers or at various kiosks and shops in the city. There are different ticket types, including single rides and daily or weekly passes. The prices may vary, so it's a good idea to check with the bus company for the latest fare information.

3. **Bus Schedules:** Bus schedules can change, and they may vary by the season, so it's advisable to check the official Libertas Dubrovnik website or at the bus stops for the latest information on routes and schedules. Buses typically run from early morning until late evening, with reduced service during the night.

4. **Buses to the Airport:** There is a regular bus service that connects the city center with Dubrovnik Airport. This is a convenient and cost-effective way to reach the airport from the city.

5. **Boat Transportation:** In addition to buses, Dubrovnik also offers boat transportation, particularly to nearby islands like

Lokrum and the Elaphiti Islands. These boats depart from the Old Town's harbor and provide scenic rides to the islands.

6. **Taxi Services:** Taxis are available in Dubrovnik, but they are generally more expensive than the bus system. Taxis can be a convenient option for travelers who prefer a direct and private mode of transportation.

7. **Parking:** If you plan to rent a car while in Dubrovnik, be aware that parking within the Old Town is very limited, and it's often easier to park in the newer parts of the city or in designated parking areas outside the Old Town. There are parking lots and garages available for a fee.

8. **Ticket Validation:** When you board a bus, make sure to validate your ticket using the machine on board. This is important, as inspectors may check for validated tickets during your journey.

9. **Bicycles:** While public transportation is the most common means of getting around, Dubrovnik is a walkable city, and you can explore the Old Town on foot. Bicycle rentals are available if you wish to explore the city and its surroundings at a more leisurely pace.

Packing Tips

1. Travel Documents:

- Passport and visa (if required)

- Driver's license (if you plan to rent a car)

- Printed or digital copies of your itinerary, hotel reservations, and travel insurance information

- Travel adapters and chargers for your devices

- A small travel wallet to keep your important documents organized

2. Clothing:

- Lightweight, breathable clothing, especially during the summer months

- Swimwear if you plan to visit the beaches

- Comfortable walking shoes for exploring the city and its attractions

- Sandals or flip-flops for the beach and casual outings

- A light jacket or sweater for cooler evenings

- Sun protection gear like a wide-brimmed hat, sunglasses, and sunscreen

- Comfortable clothes for outdoor activities, such as hiking or kayaking

- A reusable shopping bag for carrying items or groceries

- Dressier attire for evening dining if you plan to visit upscale restaurants

3. Toiletries and Personal Items:

- Toiletry bag with essentials like toothbrush, toothpaste, shampoo, conditioner, and soap

- Hairdryer, if not provided by your accommodation

- Any prescription medications and a copy of your prescriptions

- Insect repellent and antihistamines for insect bites

- First-aid kit with band-aids, pain relievers, and other essentials

- Travel-sized laundry detergent for washing clothes

- Feminine hygiene products if needed

- Beach towel and/or blanket

4. Electronics:

- Smartphone, camera, or GoPro for capturing memories

- Power bank and charging cables

- Universal travel adapter to plug in your devices

- E-reader or tablet for reading during downtime

- Headphones for entertainment during your travels

- Waterproof case or pouch for your electronics if you plan to be near the water

5. Luggage and Bags:

- A sturdy and well-organized suitcase or backpack

- A smaller daypack or backpack for day trips and carrying essentials

- Packing cubes or organizers to keep your clothing and belongings tidy

- A luggage lock for security

- A reusable water bottle to stay hydrated during your explorations

Language Phrases
Greetings and Politeness:

1. Hello - Bok (informal) / Dobar dan (formal)

2. Good morning - Dobro jutro

3. Good evening - Dobra večer

4. Good night - Laku noć

5. Please - Molim

6. Thank you - Hvala

7. Yes - Da

8. No - Ne

9. Excuse me - Oprostite

10. I'm sorry - Žao mi je

Basic Questions:

11. What is your name? - Kako se zovete? (formal) / Kako se zoveš? (informal)

12. How much does this cost? - Koliko ovo košta?

13. Where is the bathroom? - Gdje je WC?

14. Can you help me? - Možete li mi pomoći?

15. What is this? - Što je ovo?

16. Do you speak English? - Govorite li engleski?

Numbers:

17. One - Jedan

18. Two - Dva

19. Three - Tri

20. Four - Četiri

21. Five - Pet

22. Six - Šest

23. Seven - Sedam

24. Eight - Osam

25. Nine - Devet

26. Ten - Deset

Eating and Food:

27. I would like... - Ja bih...

28. Water - Voda

29. Menu - Meni

30. Breakfast - Doručak

31. Lunch - Ručak

32. Dinner - Večera

33. Coffee - Kava

34. Beer - Pivo

35. Wine – Vino

Directions and Transportation: 36. Where is...? - Gdje je...?

37. Bus station - Autobusna stanica

38. Train station - Željeznička stanica

39. Airport - Zračna luka

40. Taxi - Taxi

41. Left - Lijevo

42. Right - Desno

43. Straight - Ravno

44. Stop – Stani

Emergency Phrases: 45. Help - Pomoć

46. I need a doctor - Trebam liječnika

47. Call the police - Pozovite policiju

48. Fire - Požar

49. I'm lost - Izgubio/la sam se

50. Where is the nearest hospital? - Gdje je najbliža bolnica?

Official Dubrovnik Tourism Website: Visit the official Dubrovnik Tourism website at https://visitdubrovnik.hr/ for up-to-date information, event listings, and maps.

Dubrovnik and Neretva County Tourist Board
Email: info@visitdubrovnik.hr
Tel: +385 (0)20 324-999,
Address: Šipčine 2, 20000 Dubrovnik, Croatia

- **Online Travel Forums**: Participate in travel forums like TripAdvisor forum to seek advice, read about the experiences of fellow travelers, and ask questions.

- **Local Tour Operators**: Consider booking tours and excursions with reputable local tour operators who can provide unique experiences and insights.

Dubrovnik Museums and Galleries: Discover the official websites of Dubrovnik's museums and galleries for exhibition schedules and visitor information.

1. **Dubrovnik Museum (Cultural Historical Museum):**
   - Official Website: https://www.dumus.hr/
   - Opening Hours:
       June to September: Daily 9:00 AM - 6:00 PM
       October to May: Daily 9:00 AM - 4:00 PM

2. **Rector's Palace (Knežev dvor):**
   - Official Website: https://www.dumus.hr/
   - Opening Hours:
       June to September: Daily 9:00 AM - 6:00 PM
       October to May: Daily 9:00 AM - 4:00 PM

3. **Dubrovnik Cathedral (Katedrala Velike Gospe):**

- Official Website: https://katedraladubrovnik.hr
- Opening Hours:
  Typically open during daylight hours, but the exact schedule may vary.

4. **Franciscan Monastery and Museum (Franjevački samostan i muzej):**
   - Opening Hours:
     Summer (last Sunday /week in March - last Sunday/week in October): 9 am - 6 pm
     Working hours in winter: 9 am - 2 pm

5. **War Photo Limited:**
   - Official Website: https://www.warphotoltd.com/
   - Opening Hours:
     June to September: Daily 9:00 AM - 9:00 PM
     October to May: Daily 10:00 AM - 6:00 PM

Dubrovnik Public Transportation: Find information on public transportation, including bus schedules, at the official Libertas Dubrovnik website (https://libertasdubrovnik.com/en).

Local Language Learning Apps: To enhance your travel experience, consider using language learning apps like Duolingo or Memorize to pick up a few Croatian phrases.

History and Culture:

1. Dubrovnik, known as the "Pearl of the Adriatic," is a UNESCO World Heritage Site, celebrated for its well-preserved medieval walls and historic architecture.

2. The city was founded in the 7th century and was a powerful maritime republic in the Middle Ages.

3. The Republic of Ragusa was the historical name for Dubrovnik, and it existed for almost five centuries, maintaining its independence.

4. The city walls of Dubrovnik are up to 6 meters thick in some places and are a prominent feature in many movies and TV series, including Game of Thrones.

5. Dubrovnik has its own patron saint, St. Blaise (Sv. Vlaho), whose feast day is celebrated on February 3rd each year with a grand procession.

6. The flag of Dubrovnik is made up of two colors: red symbolizes freedom, and blue represents the sea.

7. The Sponza Palace, an important historical building in the city, houses the State Archives, where you can find valuable historical documents.

8. The Republic of Ragusa had a highly advanced legal system and was known for its progressive and humanitarian laws.

9. Shakespeare's "Twelfth Night" is believed to have premiered in Dubrovnik in the early 1600s.

10. The city's main street, Stradun (Placa), is made of gleaming white limestone, giving it a unique and beautiful appearance.

Geography and Nature:

11. Dubrovnik is located on the southern coast of Croatia, overlooking the Adriatic Sea.

12. The city is surrounded by dramatic limestone cliffs and hills, making it a stunning destination for nature enthusiasts.

13. Lokrum Island, located just off the coast, is a protected nature reserve and home to peacocks.

14. The Elaphiti Islands, including Koločep, Lopud, and Šipan, offer beautiful natural landscapes and are easily accessible from Dubrovnik.

15. The city enjoys a Mediterranean climate with warm, dry summers and mild winters.

16. Dubrovnik's clear and calm waters make it a fantastic spot for snorkeling and scuba diving.

Architecture and Landmarks:

17. The Dubrovnik Cathedral is home to a treasury containing relics, including the head of St. Blaise.

18. Fort Lovrijenac, also known as "St. Lawrence Fortress," was built to protect the city from Venetian attacks.

19. The city features numerous baroque and Renaissance buildings, including churches, palaces, and fountains.

20. The city's iconic Dubrovnik Bridge, or Franjo Tuđman Bridge, connects Dubrovnik to the mainland.

Traditions and Festivals:

21. The Dubrovnik Summer Festival is an annual cultural event featuring numerous performances, including theater, music, and dance.

22. The Dubrovnik Carnival is a vibrant and lively event celebrated in the weeks leading up to Lent.

23. The Festival of St. Blaise (Festa svetoga Vlaha) is one of the most important festivals in Dubrovnik, celebrating the city's patron saint.

24. Traditional Croatian folklore dance and music, such as the Linđo dance, are an integral part of the city's culture.

Cuisine and Dining:

25. Seafood is a staple in Dubrovnik's cuisine, with fresh catch often used in dishes like black risotto and grilled fish.

26. Traditional dishes like Peka, which involves slow-cooking meat and vegetables under an iron bell, are a culinary delight.

27. Croatian wines, especially those from the nearby Pelješac Peninsula, are highly regarded and widely enjoyed.

Economy and Trade:

28. Dubrovnik was a prosperous trading city, known for its salt, which was a valuable commodity in the Middle Ages.

29. The city had its own currency, the ducat, which was widely used in the trading of goods.

Entertainment and Media:

30. Dubrovnik has served as a filming location for many famous productions, including "Game of Thrones" and the James Bond film "From Russia with Love."

31. The Dubrovnik Film Festival showcases local and international cinema.

Transportation:

32. Dubrovnik Airport, known as Čilipi Airport, is the primary gateway to the city.

33. The Old Town of Dubrovnik is car-free, creating a unique and pedestrian-friendly atmosphere.

Tourism:

34. Tourism plays a crucial role in Dubrovnik's economy, with millions of visitors coming each year to explore its rich history and stunning landscapes.

35. The city's impressive walls extend for 1,940 meters and feature several fortresses and towers.

Cultural Heritage:

36. The traditional Dubrovnik costume is an important part of the city's cultural heritage, often worn during special events and festivals.

37. The historical Dubrovnik Republic produced its own gold coins, known as "ducati ragusei."

Linguistic Diversity:

38. In addition to Croatian, many locals in Dubrovnik also speak Italian and English, making it easier for tourists to communicate.

Maritime Heritage:

39. The city's strong maritime history is reflected in the Maritime Museum, which is located in the Old Town.

Fortified Towns:

40. Ston and Mali Ston, nearby towns known for their salt production and impressive city walls, are often included in Dubrovnik itineraries.

Stradun Paving:

41. Stradun's polished limestone paving is so slippery that the locals have a saying, "Stradun is our ice rink."

The Sweet Delight:

42. In Dubrovnik, you can try traditional desserts like Rozata, a caramel custard flan.

Religious Tolerance:

43. Dubrovnik was known for its religious tolerance and was home to multiple religious communities, including Catholics, Orthodox Christians, and Jews.

Cultural and Political Influence:

44. Dubrovnik's cultural and political influence extended to countries and regions, including Italy, the Balkans, and the Mediterranean.

The Dubrovnik Symphony Orchestra:

45. The Dubrovnik Symphony Orchestra, founded in 1923, is one of the oldest orchestras in Croatia.

The Legend of Orlando:

46. The Orlando Column, a statue of the medieval knight Orlando, was a symbol of freedom and the rule of law in the city.

Seafaring and Navigation:

47. The Maritime Museum in Dubrovnik features exhibits on seafaring, navigation, and maritime trade.

A UNESCO Treasure:

48. Dubrovnik's Old Town is a UNESCO World Heritage Site due to its well-preserved historical and cultural significance.

The City of Festivals:

49. In addition to the Dubrovnik Summer Festival, the city hosts a variety of events, including the Libertas Film Festival and Good Food Festival.

Game of Thrones Connection:

50. Dubrovnik served as the primary filming location for King's Landing in the popular TV series "Game of Thrones," attracting fans from around the world to explore the iconic settings.

NOTE

NOTE

NOTE

NOTE

NOTE

NOTE

Image Credits

While we have made every effort to properly credit all photographs used in this travel guide, we sincerely apologize for any inadvertent omissions. If you believe your photo has been used without your permission, please contact us at harrisonwalshawtravels@gmail.com right away and we will make the necessary changes.

Printed in Great Britain
by Amazon

46193225R00056